BAHAMAS: HUMAN RIGHTS

EXECUTIVE SUMMARY

The Commonwealth of The Bahamas is a constitutional, parliamentary democracy. Prime Minister Perry Christie's Progressive Liberal Party (PLP) won control of the government in May 2012 elections that international observers found to be generally free and fair. Authorities maintained effective control over the security forces. Security forces occasionally committed human rights abuses.

The most serious human rights problems were police abuse, detainee abuse (compounded by problems in processing them), a poorly functioning judicial system leading to delays in trial, and witness intimidation.

Other human rights problems included poor detention conditions; corruption; violence and discrimination against women; sexual abuse of children; and discrimination based on ethnic descent, sexual orientation, or HIV status.

The government took action against police officers and other officials accused of abuse of power, and there was not a widespread perception of impunity.

Section 1. Respect for the Integrity of the Person, Including Freedom from:

a. Arbitrary or Unlawful Deprivation of Life

There were no reports that the government or its agents committed arbitrary or unlawful killings. There were occasional reports of fatal shootings and questionable deaths of suspects in police custody. Bystanders at some shootings claimed that police were too quick to use their firearms and, in some instances, declared that police officers acted unprofessionally. Police investigated all such incidents and referred them to a coroner's court for further evaluation. In addition all deaths in police custody go before the coroner's court.

Authorities reported five fatalities in police operations through November.

On February 8, a suspect died in police custody, hours after police brought him in for questioning in connection with an armed robbery and escape. In May a Coroner's Court jury ruled that the death was an "unlawful killing." The coroner forwarded the case to the attorney general to determine whether charges or other action would be brought against the officers involved. Authorities had made no decision by November.

Although more recent data were not available, in 2011 the Coroner's Court resolved 1,278 cases and faced a backlog of 846 cases, including a few pending cases involving police shootings.

b. Disappearance

There were no reports of politically motivated disappearances.

c. Torture and Other Cruel, Inhuman, or Degrading Treatment or Punishment

The constitution prohibits torture and cruel, inhuman, and degrading treatment or punishment. At times citizens and visitors alleged instances of police abuse of criminal suspects.

On April 4, a defense attorney accused a police officer of beating her client until he confessed to a 2010 murder. She further alleged that the only evidence linking her client to the crime was his disputed confession.

Prison and Detention Center Conditions

Prison and detention center conditions generally failed to meet international standards, and conditions at Her Majesty's Prison at Fox Hill (HMP), the country's only prison, remained harsh and unsanitary for many prisoners.

Physical Conditions: HMP facilities include the remand center, remand court, maximum-security blocks, medium security and minimum security/work release units, and a separate women's unit. Overcrowding and access to adequate medical care were major problems in the men's maximum-security block. In October authorities reported the daily population of the prison and the remand center at 1,433, compared with more than 1,600 in August 2012. Minister of National Security Bernard Nottage characterized overcrowding at the prison, designed to hold 750 inmates, as "unacceptable," attributing the overcrowding to the large number of petty criminals incarcerated and to the backlog in processing at the remand center. To address overcrowding in the remand center, which stemmed from processing backlogs within the judicial system, authorities held prisoners awaiting trial in the maximum-security block. In October the prison superintendent reported the maximum-security wing of the prison held 802 inmates, which was twice the number of inmates it was built to house when constructed in 1953. Authorities generally held non-Bahamian citizens deemed to pose an escape risk in remand in the maximum-security block. Authorities estimated that 79 percent of those held in maximum security were awaiting trial.

In September authorities reported confining as many as five inmates to cells intended for one or two prisoners. Others remained in poorly ventilated and poorly lit cells that lacked regular running water. Inmates removed human waste by bucket. Authorities installed suitable waste plumbing in the maximum-security unit, but toilets were not yet in place. Authorities allowed maximum-security inmates outside for exercise four days a week for one hour per day. Medium-security and minimum-security units had running water and toilets and, in some cases, a television for prisoners to watch. Four reverse-osmosis units installed at various prison housing units allowed each inmate to extract a one gallon of potable water during exercise time each day, free of charge. In addition inmates could purchase bottled water and other beverages from the prison commissary.

Prison guards complained about conditions, including inadequate running water in the prison, repairs needed for the women's prison, and improper management of officers. They also cited the lack of a full-time dentist, failure to appoint a staff psychiatrist, incomplete perimeter walls for more than five years, and a damaged roof in need of repair in the maximum-security block; moreover, they asserted that the use of prison guards at the remand center violated the Prison Act. A formal panel reviewed the guards' complaints and determined the majority to be without merit. The damaged roof was under repair at the end of the year.

There were two inmate deaths through November. Authorities reported that both were due to natural causes.

Authorities held female prisoners at HMP in a separate building located away from the retention area for male prisoners, but still within the same area surrounded by the prison wall. On October 1, there were 45 female prisoners. Conditions were less severe and less crowded than for men; however, women did not have access to the same work-release programs available for male prisoners. Data on the number of female inmates who were awaiting trial were not available.

Authorities kept all juvenile offenders separated from adult offenders, holding remanded male juveniles in a custody block designated for juveniles only. They placed sentenced male juveniles at the medium security facility at HMP. They kept all female juveniles at the Female Housing Security Unit separated from adults.

The highest occupancy at the Carmichael Road Immigrant Detention Center through November was 214 persons in early September. Authorities converted the center, originally a school, into a detention center in the mid-1990s to accommodate the increase in number of irregular migrants. When the center initially opened, it consisted of four dormitories, each with a 50-bed capacity. Two of those dormitories burned in a 2004 fire, limiting the facility to two dormitories with capacity for 150 detainees. Drinking water was available from a tap in the facility. The dormitories were gender segregated and secured using locked gates, metal fencing, and barbed wire. When the dormitories were at maximum capacity, detention center staff utilized the floor of the main hall in the medical building to accommodate up to another 50 individuals with sleeping space. Any additional detainees slept outside. International observers noted 150 beds in the center. Authorities held parent detainees with children in the women's dormitory at the detention center. They held unaccompanied minors in the Children's Emergency Hostel and the Elizabeth Estates Children's Home.

Five Cuban detainees drew international attention when they claimed that detention center guards beat them on May 5 with batons and pipes, resulting in at least one hospitalization and various injuries. The government conducted an internal investigation and charged five Royal Bahamas Defence Force (RBDF) marines via a closed military tribunal. The proceedings continued as of November.

As of September 17, there were 90 detainees in the facility. In 2012 authorities reported that they repatriated 3,318 irregular immigrants to their home countries. That group consisted of 2,525 Haitians (2,059 males, 431 females, and 35 children) and 793 from other countries.

With the exception of the May 5 incident, authorities reported only minor complaints from detainees during the year, mostly concerning type and quantity of food. An advocacy group alleged additional assaults, including the sexual assault of a female detainee. Human rights organizations also reported that rats and mice infested the living quarters. Authorities denied some detainees the right to contact their respective embassies or consulates. None of the eight pay telephones were operational and no alternative telephone was available to detainees. Detainees did not have access to an ombudsman or other means of submitting uncensored complaints.

Administration: Generally, prisoners and detainees had reasonable access to visitors and could participate in religious observance. Some organizations providing aid, counseling services, and religious instruction had regular access to inmates. Although there was no designated ombudsman, prisoners were entitled to an audience with the superintendent or a designee upon request to lodge complaints. The superintendent was available to hear the complaints of prisoners every day of the week except Sundays. Although more recent data were not available, in 2011 authorities said that there were 20 complaints to judicial authorities concerning situations in the prison, mostly related to a desire to be placed in the day-release work program, a shortage of recreational equipment, and greater access to dental facilities. Officials stated they investigated all credible allegations. Through October 1, authorities reported 22 preliminary inquiries and investigations of staff and inmates. Alternative sentencing for nonviolent offenders was not available. The tracking of prisoners was adequate. Two prisoners escaped while receiving medical treatment at the government hospital and were later recaptured.

Independent Monitoring: Human rights organizations complained that the government did not consistently grant requests by independent human rights observers for access to HMP, Carmichael Road Detention Center, and the two juvenile centers. The government maintained additional bureaucratic procedures for some nongovernmental organizations (NGOs) to gain access to the detention center, making it difficult to visit detainees on a regular basis.

Improvements: Through October the HMP superintendent reported improvements to the water-supply system, commissary expansion, and increased entrance security in an attempt to control contraband. A new drug rehabilitation dorm held 15 inmates.

d. Arbitrary Arrest or Detention

The constitution prohibits arbitrary arrest and detention, and the government generally observed these prohibitions, although media reports occasionally accused police of arresting and detaining persons arbitrarily.

Role of the Police and Security Apparatus

The Royal Bahamas Police Force (RBPF) maintains internal security. The small RBDF is primarily responsible for external security but also provides security at the Carmichael Road Detention Center and performs some minor domestic security functions such as guarding foreign embassies and ambassadors. The Ministry of National Security oversees both the RBPF and the RBDF. In September the RBDF began augmenting the RBPF in administrative and support roles as part of a temporary anticrime initiative.

Authorities automatically placed police officers involved in shooting or killing a suspect under investigation. The Police Complaints and Corruption Branch (PCCB), which reports directly to the deputy commissioner, is responsible for investigating allegations of police brutality or other abuse. This unit determines if enough evidence of abuse or misconduct exists in a particular case to warrant disciplinary action within the police system or, in some cases, criminal prosecution by the attorney general. The PCCB had 21 staff members to process complaints against police officers.

In addition to the PCCB, an independent body – the Police Complaints Inspectorate Office (PCIO) – investigated complaints against police. The PCIO, which is composed of five citizens, meets several times per year. No information was available on the outcome of the PCIO proceedings.

As of October 1, there were 163 complaints against officers, about half of which involved assault. Other complaints included unethical behavior, property damage, unlawful arrest, stealing, missing property, causing harm, threats of harm, neglect of duty, indecent assault, and unlawful entry or search. Of these cases, authorities resolved 31 and recommended court inquiries in 13 cases.

Arrest Procedures and Treatment of Detainees

In general the authorities conducted arrests openly and, when required, obtained judicially issued warrants. Serious cases, including suspected narcotics or firearms offenses, do not require warrants where probable cause exists. The law provides that authorities must charge a suspect within 48 hours of arrest. Arrested persons appear before a magistrate within 48 hours (or by the next business day for cases arising on weekends and holidays) to hear the charges against them. Police can apply for a 48-hour extension upon simple request to the court and for longer extensions with sufficient showing of need. Some persons on remand claimed they were not brought before a magistrate within the 48-hour time frame. The government generally respected the right to a judicial determination of the legality of arrests. The constitution provides the right for those arrested or detained to retain an attorney at their own expense; volunteer legal aides were sometimes available. Minors under age 18 have the right to communicate with a parent or guardian.

There was a functioning bail system. Individuals who could not post bail were held on remand until they faced trial. Judges sometimes authorized cash bail for foreigners arrested on minor charges; however, foreign suspects generally preferred to plead guilty and pay a fine rather than pursue their right to defend themselves, in view of possible delays in court cases and harsh conditions in prison.

Pretrial Detention: Attorneys and other prisoner advocates continued to complain of excessive pretrial detention due to the failure of the criminal justice system to try even the most serious cases in a timely manner. The constitution provides that authorities may hold suspects in pretrial detention for a "reasonable period of time," which is defined as two years. As of October 1, more than 600 prisoners were awaiting trial. To address the overcrowding issue, in 2010 authorities introduced a new electronic ankle-bracelet surveillance system in which they released select suspects awaiting trial with the ankle bracelet on the understanding that the person would adhere to strict and person-specific guidelines defining allowable movement within the country. The courts were not consistent with the application of curfews or movement restrictions under the bracelet program. In October authorities monitored 430 accused persons through the ankle-bracelet system. The Ministry of National Security reported problems with the monitoring procedures after a man died in July while wearing a bracelet with no one discovering his body until several days afterward.

Authorities detained irregular immigrants, primarily Haitians, until arrangements could be made for them to leave the country or they obtained legal status. The average length of detention varied significantly by nationality, willingness of governments to accept their nationals back in a timely manner, and availability of funds to pay for repatriation. Authorities usually repatriated Haitians within one to two weeks, while they held Cubans for much longer periods. Authorities held irregular immigrants convicted of crimes other than immigration violations at HMP where, after serving their sentences, they often remained for weeks or months pending deportation.

e. Denial of Fair Public Trial

The constitution provides for an independent judiciary, and the government generally respected judicial independence. Sitting judges are not granted tenure, and some law professionals asserted that judges were incapable of rendering completely independent decisions due to lack of job security.

Trial Procedures

The constitution provides for the right to a fair trial, and an independent judiciary generally enforced this right. Procedural shortcomings, trial delays, and a significant backlog of cases in the Supreme Court were a problem.

Defendants enjoy a presumption of innocence until proven guilty and are permitted to question witnesses at trial and view government evidence. Defendants have a right to appeal. Defendants can elect to use a jury in criminal cases; serious offenses such as murder and fraud automatically go to a jury. Defendants have the right to present their own witnesses and evidence. Although defendants generally have the right to access government-held evidence and confront adverse witnesses, in some cases the law allows witnesses to testify anonymously against accused perpetrators. This law was enacted to protect witnesses from intimidation or retribution. Authorities dismissed at least three murder charges during the year because the witnesses either refused to testify or could not be located. Efforts to protect witnesses were hindered by the fact that 70 percent of citizens live within the 80 square miles that make up New Providence Island.

Defendants may hire an attorney of their choice, but the government provided legal representation only to destitute suspects charged with capital crimes, leaving large numbers of defendants without adequate legal representation. Lack of representation contributed to excessive pretrial detention, as some accused lacked the means to pursue their case toward trial.

As in previous years, a significant backlog of cases awaiting trial by the Supreme Court remained a problem. Delays reportedly lasted five years or more. The courts have not kept pace with the rise in criminal cases and remained insufficient to address the growing backlog of cases. Once cases go to trial, they were often further delayed due to poor case and court management. Examples of shortcomings included inaccurate handling or presentation of evidence and inaccurate scheduling of witnesses, jury members, and accused criminals for testimony.

Local legal professionals attributed delays to a variety of longstanding systemic problems, such as slow and limited police investigations, inefficient prosecution strategies, limited forensic capacity, lengthy legal procedures, and staff shortages in the Prosecutor's Office. The press reported that the many problems identified in a 2004 audit of the Court Reporting Unit remained unresolved. These problems included a shortage of court reporters and extensive delays in producing transcripts. According to several legal professionals, executive branch control of the budget and assignment of personnel for the judicial branch of government remained a separation of powers problem.

Political Prisoners and Detainees

There were no reports of political prisoners or detainees.

Civil Judicial Procedures and Remedies

There is an independent and impartial judiciary in civil matters, and there is access to a court to bring lawsuits seeking damages for, or cessation of, a human rights violation.

f. Arbitrary Interference with Privacy, Family, Home, or Correspondence

The constitution prohibits such actions, and the government generally respected these prohibitions.

While the law usually requires a court order for entry into or search of a private residence, a police inspector or more senior police official may authorize a search without a court order where probable cause to suspect a weapons violation or drug possession exists.

Section 2. Respect for Civil Liberties, Including:

a. Freedom of Speech and Press

The constitution provides for freedom of speech and press, and the government generally respected these rights. An independent press, a relatively effective – albeit extremely backlogged – judiciary, and a functioning democratic political system combined to promote freedom of speech and press. The independent media were active and expressed a wide variety of views without significant restriction.

Internet Freedom

There were no government restrictions on access to the internet or credible reports that the government monitored e-mail or internet chat rooms without appropriate legal authorization. The internet was widely available on New Providence and Grand Bahama islands, and the government estimated that 65 percent of the population used the internet.

Academic Freedom and Cultural Events

There were no government restrictions on academic freedom or cultural events. The Plays and Films Control Board rated and censored plays and films for public viewing.

b. Freedom of Peaceful Assembly and Association

The constitution provides for freedom of assembly and association, and the government generally respected these rights.

c. Freedom of Religion

See the Department of State's *International Religious Freedom Report* at www.state.gov/j/drl/irf/rpt.

d. Freedom of Movement, Internally Displaced Persons, Protection of Refugees, and Stateless Persons

The constitution provides for freedom of internal movement, foreign travel, emigration, and repatriation, and the government generally respected these rights. The government generally cooperated with the Office of the UN High Commissioner for Refugees (UNHCR) and other humanitarian organizations in assisting refugees and asylum seekers. The government did not systematically share its prescreening notes with the UNHCR, but it sought UNHCR advice on specific cases of concern.

Protection of Refugees

Access to Asylum: The government has not established a consistent system for providing protection to all refugees and asylum seekers. When they occurred, authorities adjudicated applications for political asylum on a case-by-case basis at the cabinet level, with advisory assistance from the UNHCR. As of October 17, the UNHCR reported 92 requests for asylum, all but one from Cuban nationals. The government recognized 12 as refugees with some cases still pending.

In August the government repatriated 24 Cuban migrants to Cuba, in spite of public offers of asylum from the Government of Panama, before the UNHCR could make a formal determination of their status. Local and international human rights observers criticized the government for failing to screen potential asylum applicants adequately, but the Ministry of Foreign Affairs reported that the UNHCR assisted such applicants. Those requesting asylum screening often lacked access to legal counsel. International human rights organizations reported that the government maintains a memorandum of understanding with the Cuban government allowing for information sharing that heightened the risk of the persecution of detainees and their families. They also claimed that the government detained Cuban migrants for excessive periods. The government asserted that trained immigration officials interviewed and adequately screened all migrants who claimed asylum.

Stateless Persons

The government has not effectively implemented laws and policies to provide certain habitual residents the opportunity to gain nationality in a timely manner and on a nondiscriminatory basis. Children born in the Bahamas to non-Bahamian parents, to an unwed Bahamian father and a non-Bahamian mother, or outside the country to a Bahamian mother and a non-Bahamian father do not acquire citizenship at birth. Bahamian-born persons of foreign heritage must apply for citizenship during a 12-month window following their 18th birthday, sometimes waiting many years for a government response. The narrow window for application, difficult documentary requirements, and long waiting times created generations of de facto stateless persons. Some commentators believed that these restrictions particularly targeted Haitians resident in the country. In 2012 then Minister of Foreign Affairs and Immigration Brent Symonette stated that 2,590 applications for citizenship were approved between May 2007 and the close of 2011. It was not clear how many applications were submitted, and how many of those approved were from applicants of Haitian descent.

There were no reliable estimates of the number of de facto stateless persons. The government asserted that a number of "stateless" individuals had a legitimate claim to Haitian citizenship but refused to pursue it out of fear of deportation or loss of future claim to Bahamian citizenship. Such persons often faced waiting periods of several years for the government to decide on their nationality applications and, as a result, lacked proper documentation to secure employment, housing, access to health services, and other public facilities during this period.

Individuals born in the country to non-Bahamian parents were eligible to apply for certificates of identification that entitled them to work, allowed access to public high school-level education, and a fee-for-service health-care insurance program. Human rights advocates criticized the health insurance program as having unrealistic payment requirements that limited widespread access. Authorities allowed individuals born in the country to non-Bahamian parents to pay the tuition rate for Bahamian students when enrolled in college and while waiting for their request for citizenship to be processed.

Section 3. Respect for Political Rights: The Right of Citizens to Change Their Government

The constitution provides citizens with the right to change their government peacefully, and citizens exercised this right through periodic, free, and fair elections based on universal suffrage.

Elections and Political Participation

Recent Elections: A general election in May 2012 resulted in a victory for the opposition PLP and a change of government. Prime Minister Perry Gladstone Christie took office after defeating the Free National Movement (FNM) party led by former Prime Minister Hubert Ingraham. Christie had previously served as prime minister from 2002 to 2007. The PLP won 29 of the 38 parliamentary seats, with 48 percent of the popular vote. The FNM won the remaining nine seats. Ingraham resigned his seat shortly after his party lost the elections, and a PLP candidate won the seat, bringing the total PLP parliamentary seats to 30.

In advance of the elections, the Ingraham government revised its electoral legislation to allow official election observers to participate in the electoral process for the first time. Election observers from the Organization of American States and foreign embassies found the elections to be generally free and fair. After the election the FNM and some media alleged that persons associated with that party were "victimized" when they were dismissed from government jobs following the change in government.

Participation by Women and Minorities: Five women served in the 38-seat House of Assembly. The prime minister appointed four women to the 21-member cabinet and five women to the 16-seat Senate, one of whom was its president. Nine of the 20 permanent secretaries were women.

Authorities did not collect information on racial background, but there were members of minorities in prominent positions in parliament and the cabinet.

Section 4. Corruption and Lack of Transparency in Government

The law provides criminal penalties for official corruption, and the government generally implemented these laws effectively. There were some reports of government corruption during the year.

Corruption: There is no government agency specifically responsible for monitoring allegations of government corruption. Such allegations are reported to the commissioner of police. When allegations of corruption are brought to the attention of the House of Assembly, the group may elect to constitute an investigative committee to inquire into the matter further.

Whistleblower Protection: The law does not provide protection to public or private employees for making internal disclosures or lawful public disclosures of evidence of illegality.

Financial Disclosure: The Public Disclosure Act requires senior public officials, including senators and members of parliament, to declare their assets, income, and liabilities on an annual basis. The declaration applies to spouses and dependent family members. The government publishes a summary of the individual declarations. There is no independent verification of the submitted data, and the rate of annual submission is weak except in election years.

Public Access to Information: As of October the government had not issued implementing regulations nor conducted any public information/education campaigns conducted about the Freedom of Information Act approved in February 2012. The act provides access to government information upon request from citizens and permanent residents, except for the following: reports that would compromise the country's security, confidential communication to the government by or on behalf of a foreign jurisdiction or international organization, information that could jeopardize the security of a prison, and cabinet papers. The act stipulates a fine of 10,000 Bahamian dollars (B$) ($10,000) for anyone who contravenes the legislation but does not include an implementation date.

Section 5. Governmental Attitude Regarding International and Nongovernmental Investigation of Alleged Violations of Human Rights

A number of domestic and international human rights groups generally operated without government restriction, investigating and publishing their findings on human rights cases. Government officials usually were cooperative and responsive to their views.

Government Human Rights Bodies: A governmental commissioner with ombudsman-like duties enjoyed the government's cooperation and was considered effective.

Section 6. Discrimination, Societal Abuses, and Trafficking in Persons

The constitution prohibits discrimination on the basis of race, place of origin, political opinion, or creed, and the government generally enforced these prohibitions. The constitution and the law contain provisions that discriminate against women.

The country consists of 700 islands and cays, 12 of which are significantly inhabited. Information in this report reflects the situation in the highly populated areas on New Providence and Grand Bahama. Limited information was available from other lesser-populated islands.

Women

Rape and Domestic Violence: Rape is illegal, but the law does not protect against spousal rape, except if the couple is separating, in the process of divorce, or if there is a restraining order in place. The maximum penalty for an initial rape conviction is seven years; the maximum for subsequent rape convictions is life imprisonment. In practice, however, the maximum sentence was 14 years. As of October 1, authorities reported 83 rapes, compared with 97 in all of 2012. Authorities initiated 20 prosecutions for rape.

Violence against women continued to be a serious, widespread problem. Through October police reported receiving 375 domestic violence cases. In November the Bahamas Crisis Center (BCC) told the media that the level of domestic violence had exceeded 1,200 cases annually. In 2012 the police commissioner reported that many of the killings were related to domestic violence, and another official indicated that 45 percent of all homicides over the last 20 years could be attributed to domestic violence. Assailants killed eight women through November, compared with 10 in all of 2012.

Domestic abuse law prohibits domestic violence as a crime separate from assault and battery, and the government generally enforced the law. Women's rights groups cited some reluctance on the part of law enforcement authorities to intervene in domestic disputes. The BCC worked with police by providing them with a counselor referral service to utilize when encountering rape victims. The BCC operated a toll-free hotline in New Providence and Grand Bahama, run by trained volunteers to respond to emergency calls 24 hours a day. Government and private women's organizations continued public awareness campaigns highlighting the problems of abuse and domestic violence. The Ministry of Labor and Social Development's Department of Social Services, in partnership with a private organization, operated a safe house to assist female survivors. The ministry's Bureau of Women's Affairs was responsible for promoting and protecting women's rights.

Sexual Harassment: The law prohibits criminal "quid pro quo" sexual harassment and authorizes penalties of up to B$5,000 ($5,000) and a maximum of two years' imprisonment. There were no reports of workplace sexual harassment during the year. Civil rights advocates complained that criminal prohibitions were not enforced effectively and that civil remedies, including a prohibition on "hostile environment" sexual harassment, were needed.

Reproductive Rights: Couples and individuals generally could decide freely and responsibly the number, spacing, and timing of their children and were not subject to discrimination, coercion, or violence regarding these choices. Access to family planning was universally available to persons age 18 and older and to younger persons with the consent of a parent or guardian. Authorities removed pregnant teens from government educational institutions and placed them in a special school operated by the Providing Access to Continued Education Foundation until after the birth of their children. The Maternal and Child Health Unit of the Ministry of Health provided information pamphlets on maternal and child health to clinics. A government website provided information for maternal and child health-care services provided by various clinics throughout the country. Women had access to maternal health services. According to the latest UN data, in 2010 skilled personnel attended 99 percent of births, and 98 percent of mothers received prenatal and postpartum care. Services were available on a nondiscriminatory basis, although some irregular immigrants did not receive postpartum care because they had no fixed address.

Discrimination: The law does not provide women with the same right as men to transmit citizenship to their foreign-born spouses. The law also makes it easier for men with foreign spouses than for women with foreign spouses to transmit citizenship to their children but more difficult for unmarried men (even if able to prove paternity). The law does not include gender as a basis for protection from discrimination. Women were generally free of economic discrimination, and the law provides for equal pay for equal work.

Children

Birth Registration: Children born to non-Bahamian parents or to an unwed Bahamian father and a non-Bahamian mother do not automatically acquire citizenship. Legitimate children acquire citizenship at birth, provided at least one parent is Bahamian. In the cases of unwed parents, the child takes the citizenship of the mother. In any case, children born in the Bahamas may make application for citizenship upon reaching their 18th birthday. There is universal birth registration: all births must be registered within 21 days of delivery. All residents, regardless of immigration status, had free access to education and social programs.

Child Abuse: Both the government and civic organizations conducted public education programs aimed at child abuse and appropriate parenting behavior; however, child abuse and neglect remained serious problems. The RBPF operated a hotline regarding missing or exploited children. The Child Protection Act of 2007 included increased penalties for child abuse, mandatory reporting to police of all forms of child abuse, a provision for fathers of children born out of wedlock to pursue custody of the children, and a provision for mothers of children born out of wedlock to pursue maintenance for those children up to age 18.

The Ministry of Social Services reported 495 cases of child abuse through September. In addition the RBPF hotline reported 131 cases, including 25 reports of sexual abuse. Authorities acknowledged the system of tracking these statistics was not reliable, and the actual number of cases was likely much higher.

The law requires all persons having contact with a child they believe to have been physically or sexually abused to report their suspicions to the police. The penalties for rape of a minor are the same penalties as those for rape of an adult. While a victim's consent is insufficient defense against allegations of statutory rape, it is sufficient defense if an individual can demonstrate that the accused had "reasonable cause to believe that the victim was above 16 years of age," provided the accused was under age 18. In 2012 Social Services reported 112 of cases of adults having unlawful sexual intercourse with children age 15 and younger.

Sexual exploitation of children through incestuous relationships occurred, and anecdotal reports continued to suggest that this was a particular problem outside Nassau. The Ministry of Social Services may remove children from abusive situations if a court deems it necessary. The ministry provided services to abused and neglected children through a public-private center for children, the public hospital family-violence program, and the Bahamas Crisis Center.

Forced and Early Marriage: The legal minimum age for marriage is 18, although girls may marry at 16 and boys at 17 with parental permission.

Sexual Exploitation of Children: The minimum age for consensual sex is 16 years. The law considers any association or exposure of a child to prostitution or a prostitution house as cruelty, neglect, or mistreatment of a child. Additionally, the offense of having sex with a minor carries a penalty of life imprisonment. Child pornography is against the law. A person who produces it is liable to life imprisonment; dissemination or possession of it calls for a penalty of 20 years' imprisonment.

Institutionalized Children: The Department of Social Services is responsible for abandoned children up to 18 years of age but had very limited resources at its disposal. The government found foster homes for some children, and the government hospital housed children with physical disabilities when authorities could not find foster homes or the children needed care beyond their parents' resources. Independent human rights observers reported that the government did not consistently approve access requests to the Elizabeth Estates Children's Home and the Bilney Lane Children's Home.

International Child Abductions: The country is a party to the 1980 Hague Convention on the Civil Aspects of International Child Abduction. For information see the Department of State's report on compliance at http://travel.state.gov/abduction/resources/congressreport/congressreport_4308.html as well as country-specific information at http://travel.state.gov/abduction/country/country_5957.html.

Anti-Semitism

There were no reports of anti-Semitic acts. The local Jewish community numbered approximately 200 persons.

Trafficking in Persons

See the Department of State's *Trafficking in Persons Report* at www.state.gov/j/tip.

Persons with Disabilities

There is no specific law protecting persons with physical or mental disabilities from discrimination in employment, education, access to health care, or the provision of other state services. Provisions in other legislation address the rights of persons with disabilities, including a prohibition of discrimination on the basis of disability. Although the law mandates access for persons with physical disabilities in new public buildings, authorities rarely enforced this requirement, and very few buildings and public facilities were accessible to persons with disabilities. Advocates for persons with disabilities complained of widespread job discrimination and general apathy on the part of private employers and political leaders toward the need for training and equal opportunity. In one case authorities denied access to public educational facilities for a mentally sound child with only physical limitations confining him to a wheelchair. The Education Act affords equal access for students, but only as resources permit, with this decision made by individual schools. On family islands, children with special needs often sat in the back of classes because resources were not available.

The Disability Division within the Ministry of Labor and Social Development reported providing the following services during the year: disability allowances to persons with disabilities; financial assistance to procure prosthetics, wheelchairs, hearing aids, and other assistive devices; regular prosthetic committee meetings; annual government grants to NGOs serving the community of persons with disabilities; crisis intervention counseling; and Braille classes.

In November the Department of Social Services reported there were 10,138 persons with disabilities (5,250 males and 4,888 females).

A mix of government and private residential and nonresidential institutions provided education, training, counseling, and job placement services for adults and children with both physical and mental disabilities.

National/Racial/Ethnic Minorities

The country's racial and ethnic groups generally coexisted in a climate of peace, but anti-Haitian prejudice and resentment regarding Haitian immigration was widespread. According to unofficial estimates, between 40,000 and 80,000 residents were Haitians or persons of Haitian descent, making them the largest ethnic minority. Many persons of Haitian origin lived in shantytowns with limited sewage and garbage services, law enforcement, or other infrastructure. The conditions of the shantytowns varied greatly from one to the next and from island to island. For example, a shantytown in Abaco referred to as "The Mud" consisted of several hundred numbered houses with limited electricity, water, gas, and sewage connections. In contrast, a number of shantytowns on New Providence and other islands consisted of houses built from trash and leftover building materials, with little organization, infrastructure, or sanitation measures in place. Fires frequently broke out in Haitian shantytowns in Nassau. Authorities generally granted Haitian children access to education and social services, but interethnic tensions and inequities persisted. The Haitian community was characterized by high poverty, high unemployment, and poor health conditions. Haitians generally had difficulty in securing citizenship, residence, or work permits.

Members of the Haitian community complained of discrimination in the job market, specifically that identity and work-permit documents were controlled by employers seeking leverage by threat of deportation. Some also complained of tactics used by immigration officials in raids of Haitian or suspected Haitian communities. Government actions to address these communities often met political resistance, as many Bahamians tended to employ Haitians as cheap labor.

Societal Abuses, Discrimination, and Acts of Violence Based on Sexual Orientation and Gender Identity

Societal discrimination against lesbian, gay, bisexual, and transgender (LGBT) individuals occurred, with some persons reporting job and housing discrimination based upon sexual orientation. Although same-sex sexual activity between consenting adults is legal, the law defines the age of consent for same-sex couples as 18, compared with 16 for heterosexual couples. No domestic legislation addresses the human rights concerns of LGBT persons. LGBT NGOs can openly operate in the country. The 2006 Constitutional Review Commission found that sexual orientation did not deserve protection against discrimination. LGBT NGOs reported that LGBT persons faced some discrimination in employment, and victims were frustrated at the lack of legal recourse.

Other Societal Violence or Discrimination

Stigma and employment discrimination against persons with HIV/AIDS were high, but there were no reports of violence against persons with HIV/AIDS. Children with HIV/AIDS also faced discrimination, and authorities often did not tell teachers that a child was HIV-positive for fear of verbal abuse from both educators and peers. The government maintained a home for orphaned children infected with HIV/AIDS.

An independent facility known as the All Saints Camp operated as a hospice for approximately 60 HIV-infected individuals, using the individuals' government and family proceeds to fund its expenses. Those in contact with the camp alleged extreme neglect of the HIV-infected individuals living at the camp, ranging from non-nutritious and irregular meals to improper or lack of basic medical care. The administrator of the camp reported that it did not employ nurses or staff and that sick individuals living there took care of themselves or employed their own visiting nurses. Living conditions were generally unsanitary, although the facility improved wheelchair accessibility during the year.

Section 7. Worker Rights

a. Freedom of Association and the Right to Collective Bargaining

The law, including applicable statues and regulations, provides for the right of workers to form and join independent unions, participate in collective bargaining, and conduct legal strikes, and it prohibits antiunion discrimination. Members of the police force, defense force, fire brigade, and prison guards may not organize or join unions. In May an amendment to the Industrial Relations Act removed the ability of employers to have union recognition revoked if the parties do not reach a collective agreement after 12 months. The law can compel employers to reinstate workers illegally fired for union activity.

The government did not consistently enforce labor laws, and enforcement of remedies and penalties was weak. There was no information on the adequacy of enforcement resources. Fines varied widely by case and were not sufficient to deter violations. On October 7 the Ministry of Labor and National Insurance reported 723 labor violation complaints since January, and stated that it had 14 officers who resolved the majority of these cases in a timely manner. By law, labor disputes must first be filed with the ministry and if not resolved, they are transferred to an industrial tribunal, which determines penalties (fines) and remedies, up to a maximum of 26 weeks of an employee's pay. The tribunal's decision is final and can be appealed in court only on a strict question of law. Authorities reported a case backlog of up to three years at the tribunal.

Freedom of association and the right to collective bargaining were generally respected. There were reports that some employers utilized individual contracts instead of collective bargaining, and one employer dismissed a union shop steward, reportedly without justification, during the year. The Ministry of Labor and National Insurance reported that it did not receive any reports of threats of violence targeting union leaders by employers. Unions operated without government interference. The government appointed an experienced trade unionist to the ministry to streamline the collective bargaining process. Workers occasionally filed disputes with the authorities involving "union-busting" charges, specifically in the financial services sector.

b. Prohibition of Forced or Compulsory Labor

The law prohibits all forms of forced or compulsory labor.

The government did not consistently enforce the law. There was no information on the adequacy of resources, inspections, and remediation. Penalties for forced labor ranged from three to 10 years and were sufficiently stringent to deter violations. The Ministry of Labor and National Insurance received no reports of forced labor during the year. Local NGOs noted that exploited workers often did not report their circumstances to government officials for fear of deportation and lack of education about available resources. Officials investigated four reports of forced labor in 2012 and, in some cases, charged the perpetrators with lesser crimes.

Undocumented migrants were vulnerable to forced labor, especially in domestic servitude and in the agriculture sector. There were reports that noncitizen laborers, often of Haitian origin, were vulnerable to forced labor and suffered abuses at the hands of their employers, who were responsible for endorsing their work permits on an annual basis. Specifically, local sources indicated that employers reportedly obtained B$1,000 ($1,000) work permits for noncitizen employees and then required them to "work off" the permit fee over the course of their employment or otherwise risk losing the permit and their ability to work legally within the country.

Also see the Department of State's *Trafficking in Persons Report* at
www.state.gov/j/tip.

c. Prohibition of Child Labor and Minimum Age for Employment

The law prohibits the employment of children under age 14 for industrial work or
work during school hours. Children under age 16 may not work at night. A young
person (between ages 14 and 18) may work outside of school hours under the
following conditions: (a) in a school day, for not more than three hours; (b) in a
school week for not more than 24 hours; (c) in a nonschool day, for not more than
eight hours; (d) in a nonschool week, for not more than 40 hours. An exception
exists for "packaging boys" at grocery stores who were as young as 12 years of age
and may work no more than three hours after school. The law prohibits persons
younger than age 18 from engaging in dangerous work including construction,
mining, and road building. There was no legal minimum age for employment in
other sectors. Occupational health and safety restrictions apply to all younger
workers.

The government generally enforced the law, but there were limited resources and
inspections, with labor inspectors periodically sent to stores and businesses. The
Ministry of Labor reported no severe violations of child labor laws, although
inspectors reported several instances of children working in small merchant
businesses or excess hours in grocery stores. The penalty for violations of child
labor law is a fine between B$1,000 and B$1,500 ($1,000-$1,500). This punitive
action appeared sufficient to deter violations.

d. Acceptable Conditions of Work

The minimum wage was B$4.00 ($4.00) per hour for hourly workers, B$30 ($30)
per day for daily workers, and B$175 ($175) per week for weekly paid workers.
Since 2009 the official poverty level has been considered B$2,863 ($2,863) a year.

The law provides for a 40-hour workweek, a 24-hour rest period, and time-and-a-
half payment for hours worked beyond the standard workweek. The law stipulates
paid annual holidays and prohibits compulsory overtime. The law does not place a
cap on overtime. The government set health and safety standards appropriate to
the industries. According to the Ministry of Labor and National Insurance, the law
protects all workers, including migrant workers, in areas including wages, working
hours, working conditions, and occupational and safety standards. Workers did not

have the right to refuse to work under hazardous conditions, and legal standards did not cover undocumented and informal economy workers.

The ministry was responsible for enforcing labor laws, including the minimum wage, and had a team of five inspectors that conducted on-site visits to enforce occupational health and safety standards and investigate employee concerns and complaints, although inspections occurred infrequently. The ministry normally announced inspection visits in advance, and employers generally cooperated with inspectors to implement safety standards. It was uncertain whether these inspections were effective in enforcing health and safety standards. The government did not levy fines for noncompliance, but occasionally forced a work stoppage. Working conditions varied, and mold was a problem in schools and government facilities.

Authorities reported two workplace fatalities in 2012, the latest year for which data were available. The government did not require reporting on workplace accidents.